Logic Problems
for
Money Minds

HARRIMAN HOUSE LTD
43 Chapel Street
Petersfield
Hampshire
GU32 3DY
GREAT BRITAIN

Tel: +44 (0)1730 233870
Fax: +44 (0)1730 233880
Email: enquiries@harriman-house.com
Website: www.harriman-house.com

First published in Great Britain in 2003, reprinted in 2006
Copyright Harriman House Ltd
Published by Harriman House Ltd
The right of Philip Jenks to be identified as the author has been asserted
in accordance with the Copyright, Design and Patents Act 1988.

ISBN: 1-897-59796-7
ISBN 13: 9-781897-597965

British Library Cataloguing in Publication Data
A CIP catalogue record for this book can be obtained from the British Library.

Printed and bound by Biddles Ltd, Kings Lynn, Norfolk.

Introduction

Warren Buffett, the world's most successful investor, posed the following question to shareholders in one of his Berkshire Hathaway annual reports:

"How many legs does a dog have if you call its tail a leg?"

If you said 5, go to the back of the class. The answer is 4. "Just because you *call* its tail a leg," says Buffett, "doesn't mean it *is* a leg."

He used the riddle as an allegory for accounting shenanigans. When a company says it has made "£50 million profit", its claim should be regarded critically. Accounting rules may allow a finance director to declare X as profit, but that doesn't mean X is profit. As the saying goes, 'Profit is a matter of opinion. Cash is a matter of fact'.

The conundrums, tests and tricks in this book are in the same spirit as Buffett's dog riddle. They are meant to entertain and educate. Some are straight numeracy tests, some are word plays, some are logic traps and some require lateral thinking. A few of them are easy. Most demand some mental exertion. One was devised by Einstein.

If you have comments on any of the questions or answers in this book, or suggestions for future editions, please visit the following website:

www.harriman-house.com/logicproblems

Alternatively, email us on editorial@harriman-house.com. If we use material which you send to us, we will be sure to credit your genius, alongside Einstein's, in the next edition.

The scoring system

The questions in this book vary in difficulty. The more difficult the question, the more points you can win. The maximum number of points you can win on a question is written at the bottom of the relevant answer page inside a grey box. The empty box to the left is where you write in the number of points you have won.

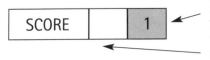

- Award yourself maximum points if you get the answer right *and* your reasoning is correct.

- Award yourself **zero** points if you get the answer wrong *and* your reasoning is completely wrong.

- Award yourself points **between zero and the maximum** if you get the answer right using the wrong reasoning, or if you get the answer wrong but your reasoning is on the right track. (As with maths exams, it is more important to use the right reasoning than it is to get the right answer.)

Add up all your points and refer to page 85 to see what this reveals about your powers of logical thinking!

Acknowledgements

The questions on pages 1, 41, 45, 61 and 63 first appeared in *Heard on the Street* by Timothy Falcon Crack, and are reproduced with his permission. *Heard on the Street* contains over 130 quantitative questions collected from actual investment banking, investment management and options trading job interviews.

This book is available from www.global-investor.com with more details available at www.investmentbankingjobinterviews.com.

Q1 Matching socks

Facts

Your bedroom sock drawer contains eight red socks and eleven blue socks that are otherwise identical. The light is broken in your bedroom, and you must select your socks in the dark.

Challenge

What is the minimum number of socks you need to take out of your drawer and carry into your (well-lit) living room to guarantee that you have with you at least one matching pair to choose from?

Reproduced from *Heard on the Street* with the permission of Timothy Falcon Crack

A₁

You need to grab three socks. Two of them might be different colours, but the third will have to match one of the first two - giving you a matching pair.

SCORE		2

Q_2 Divide and rule

Of the following numbers, which is (are) divisible by 8?

- 76
- 152
- 246

A₂

All three numbers are divisible by 8. Only 152 is evenly divisible by 8, but that wasn't the question.

| SCORE | | 2 |

4

Q3 The gold standard

Facts

A consultant for the treasury division of a bank has been retained by your firm for 7 days. Because of recent currency fluctuations, he insists on being paid every day, in gold. His fee is 1 inch of gold per day. You have just procured a 7-inch bar of gold of the right thickness to pay for the 7-day engagement.

Challenge

Making *only two* cuts to the bar of gold, to minimise gold dust waste, how can you ensure that at the end of each day he has in his possession the number of inches of gold that corresponds to the number of days worked?

A₃

Firstly, cut the 7-inch bar 1 and 3 inches along, leaving pieces of 1 inch, 2 inches and 4 inches. Then pay him as follows:

Day	Action	You have pieces	He has pieces	He has total
1	give him the 1-inch piece	4 + 2	1	1
2	give the 2-inch piece, take back the 1-inch	4 + 1	2	2
3	give the 1-inch piece	4	1 + 2	3
4	give the 4-inch piece, take back the 1 and 2-inch	1 + 2	4	4
5	give the 1-inch piece	2	4 + 1	5
6	give the 2-inch piece, take back the 1-inch	1	4 + 2	6
7	give the 1-inch piece	no pieces	4 + 2 + 1	7

SCORE	4

Q4 The janitor's dilemma

Facts

You are the janitor of a new hotel. The proprietor has asked you to buy numbers to fix to the doors of the rooms. There are 100 rooms in the hotel, numbered 1-100.

Challenge

How many number 9s do you need for the doors?

A4

You need twenty 9s.

The rooms which need a 9 on the door are:

9, 19, 29, 39, 49, 59, 69, 79, 89, 90, 91, 92, 93, 94, 95, 96, 97, 98, 99

with room 99 needing two of them.

SCORE		2

Q5 Neighbourhood watch

Facts

You have been told that the quickest way to put a sound barrier between your property and that of a noisy neighbour is to plant a row of leylandii trees. According to a friend, leylandii saplings double in height each year until they reach their maximum height after eight years.

Challenge

Assuming your friend knows what he's talking about, how many years would the leylandii trees take to reach *half* their maximum height?

A₅

They would take 7 years to reach half their maximum height.
To see why, assume that the saplings are planted on 1st January 2004
when they are 6 inches high. Their growth would be as follows:

After 1 year	1ft
After 2 years	2ft
After 3 years	4ft
After 4 years	8ft
After 5 years	16ft
After 6 years	32ft
After 7 years	64ft
After 8 years	128ft

If the maximum height is 128ft, then half the
maximum height is 64ft.

They reached 64ft after 7 years (not 4!).

SCORE		2

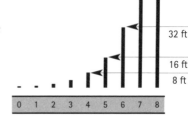

Years elapsed

Q6 Picking up cigarette ends

Facts

A homeless street-dweller can make a completely new cigarette out of every 4 cigarette ends he finds.

Challenge

If he collects 32 ends one morning, having started with none, how many whole cigarettes can he smoke that day?

A₆

He can smoke 10 cigarettes that day.

How to work it out

Initially, he can make 8 new cigarettes out of the 32 ends.

After smoking those 8, he is left with 8 'new' ends, from which he can fashion 2 further cigarettes, making 10 in total. The last two cigarettes he makes generate 2 ends when smoked, but that is not enough to make an eleventh cigarette.

SCORE		3

Q7 Scatterbrain

Facts

Scatterbrain the Treasurer had forgotten how many gold, silver and bronze coins were kept in the city vaults. He asked the three guards, each of whom guarded one type of coin, how many they had in their charge. Unfortunately, the best that he could get from each was a statement about the numbers of coins in the other two vaults.

- Dimwit, who was guarding the gold coins, said there were 3,000 silver and 5,000 bronze coins.

- Beefbrain, who was guarding the bronze coins, said there were 4,000 gold and 3,000 silver coins.

- Thickplank, who was guarding the silver coins, said there were 3,000 gold and 5,000 bronze coins.

Unfortunately, only one guard was telling the truth; each of the other two stating at least one false amount.

Challenge

If there were 12,000 coins altogether, how many of each type were there?

There were 3,000 gold coins, 4,000 silver coins and 5,000 bronze coins.

How to work it out

Assume each of the guard's statements to be true in turn, and examine the consequences:

- Dimwit said that there were 3,000 silver coins, and 5,000 bronze coins. If this was true, there must be 4,000 gold coins (because we know there are 12,000 in all). However, those numbers would make Beefbrain's statement true as well, and since we know that only *one* guard was telling the truth, Dimwit's statement cannot be true.

- Beefbrain said that there were 4,000 gold coins and 3,000 silver coins. If this was true, there must be 5,000 bronze coins. Again, if true, this would make Dimwit's statement true, so on the 'only-one-guard-is-telling-the-truth' rule, Beefbrain's statement must be false.

- That leaves Thickplank. He said that there were 3,000 gold coins and 5,000 bronze coins. If true, there would have to be 4,000 silver coins. On those numbers, the other two guards' statements are false. Thickplank is the honest guard.

SCORE	4

Q8 The European Community (Einstein's question!)

In the diplomatic community in Brussels, there are 5 houses painted in 5 different colours, each owned by a person of different nationality. Each owner drinks a certain type of beverage, smokes a certain brand of cigar and keeps a certain pet. Using the clues below can you determine who owns the fish?

- The Briton lives in a red house.
- The green house owner drinks coffee.
- The Swede keeps dogs as pets.
- The owner of the yellow house smokes Dunhill.
- The green house is on the left of the white house.
- The owner who smokes Blue Master drinks beer.
- The person who smokes Pall Mall rears birds.
- The Norwegian lives next to the blue house.
- The Norwegian lives in the first house.
- The Dane drinks tea.
- The German smokes Prince.
- The man who smokes Blend has a neighbour who drinks water.
- The man who keeps horses lives next to the man who smokes Dunhill.
- The man living in the middle house drinks milk.
- The man who smokes Blend lives next to the one who keeps cats.

A8

The German owns the fish. The table below shows the 5 houses, their colours and the proclivities of their owners.

	House 1	House 2	House 3	House 4	House 5
Nationality	Norwegian	Danish	British	German	Swedish
House colour	yellow	blue	red	green	white
Beverage	water	tea	milk	coffee	beer
Cigar brand	Dunhill	Blend	Pall Mall	Prince	Blue Master
Pet	cats	horses	birds	fish	dogs

There is no short cut to this answer. It's just a case of working through the clues and filling in the grid.

SCORE		8

Q9 Beware the croc!

Would you rather a crocodile attack you or an alligator?

A9

If you've got any sense, you would rather the crocodile attack the alligator than you.

SCORE		1

Q10 Fruit salad

Facts

A wholesaler delivers three boxes of fruit to a High Street grocer, each one with a label stuck on it. One label says 'Apples & Bananas', one says 'Apples' and one says 'Bananas'. As the driver unloads the boxes, he tells the grocer that the labels are, unfortunately, on the wrong boxes. He promises, though, that one box does contain only apples, one contains only bananas and the other contains both apples and bananas. He also says that the grocer will be able to deduce which label belongs on which box by selecting one piece of fruit from one box, without even looking inside the box and without opening the others.

Challenge

Which box should the grocer take a piece of fruit from in order to work out which label belongs to which box?

A₁₀

The grocer should take a piece of fruit from the box labelled 'Apples & Bananas'.

- If the piece of fruit is an apple, it must be the apples box and should have the 'Apples' label on it. It can't be the apples & bananas box, because he's been told that none of the labels are correct. The box with the 'Bananas' label must then be the box containing apples *and* bananas, and the box with the 'Apples' label must be the box containing bananas.

- If the piece of fruit is a banana, it must be the bananas box and should have the 'Bananas' label on it. The box with the 'Apples' label must then be the box containing apples *and* bananas, and the box with the 'Bananas' label must be the box containing apples.

SCORE		4

Q11 Cubes

A 3 inch unpainted wooden cube is painted bright green on all its sides and allowed to dry. The cube is then cut into 27 smaller cubes of 1 inch square. All the 1 inch cubes are collected and thrown like dice onto a flat surface. What is the probability that all the top facing surfaces are painted green?

A₁₁

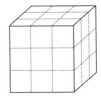

The probability is zero.

Reasoning

When cut up, there are 27 1-inch cubes.

One of them, the one at the very centre, has no painted sizes. All 6 of its sides will have been untouched by the painting of the outside of the 3 inch cube. Hence, when the 1 inch cubes are rolled, there is a 100% probability that at least one (the core cube) will land with an unpainted side facing up. Which means there is a 0% probability that they will all land with green sides up.

SCORE		3

Q12 Barrels

Answer quickly.

Starting with an empty barrel, which happens first when filling it?

- 2/3 full
- 1/4 empty
- 1/2 full
- 3/4 empty

A₁₂

3/4 empty; since 3/4 empty means 1/4 full.

After that, the order is:

1/2 full

2/3 full

1/4 empty

SCORE		1

Q13 Who got the runs?

Facts

During a cricket match, the total number of runs scored by the first six batsmen was 103. The first batsman scored half the runs of the second batsman, who in turn scored 6 runs less than the third batsman. The third batsman scored two thirds of the runs scored by the fourth batsman. The fifth batsman managed to score the same number of runs as the difference between the first and fourth batsman's runs. The sixth batsman scored 14 less than the fifth batsman.

Challenge

How many runs did the sixth batsman score?

A13

The sixth batsman scored 9 runs. The scores of all six batsmen were:

Batsman 1 – *7 runs, 2 – 14 runs, 3 – 20 runs, 4 – 30 runs, 5 – 23 runs,* and 6 – *9 runs.*

To work it out, assume the first batsman scored *n* runs. On that basis, the scores of all 6 were:

1	2	3	4	5	6	Total
n	(2n)	(2n + 6)	((2n+6) x 1.5)	(((2n+6) x 1.5) - n)	((((2n+6) x 1.5) - n) - 14)	103

This can be simplified as 5n + 6 + 3n + 9 +2n + 9 + 2n -5 = 103
12n +19 = 103
12n = 84
n = 7

Once you know n = 7, you can calculate batsman 6's score as
((((14 + 6) x 1.5) - 7) - 14) which is 9.

SCORE		4

Q14 Always check your change

Facts

Susan went to the bank to cash a cheque. She collected her money, went to the newsagent next door, and spent 68p. At that point, she realised that the bank teller had made a mistake when handing over the cash. He had transposed the pounds with the pence. Susan now had exactly twice the value of the original cheque in cash in her hand.

Challenge

What was the value of the original cheque?

A14

The cheque cashed by Susan was for £10.21. Since the bank teller muddled the pounds up with the pennies, she received £21.10. After spending 68p in the newsagent, she had £20.42 left, which is exactly twice the value of the cheque.

How to work it out

Assume that the value of the original cheque was x pounds and y pence. On that basis:

$100y + x - 68 = 2 (100x + y)$
$100y + x - 68 = 200x + 2y$
$98y - 199x = 68$

Because x and y can only be integers in the range 0-99, you can solve this equation by plugging in values for x=1, 2, 3, etc. and seeing what y turns out to be. For values of x from 1-9, y is not an integer, so those values cannot be right. When you get to x=10, however, the equation becomes: 98y - 1990 = 68. This resolves to y = 21, which makes the original cheque £10.21. Since 10 is the *only* value for x between 1 and 99 for which y is also an integer, this must be the correct answer.

SCORE		5

Q15 You bet!

While in a casino, you are approached by a stranger who says:

"I bet you £1 that if you give me £2, I will give you £3 in return."

Should you accept the bet?

A15

No! If you take the bet, you have to give him £2 to 'activate' the bet. If he refuses to give you £3, he loses the bet and hands you £1 in winnings. He has come out £1 on top. and you have lost £1.

SCORE		1

Q16 A question of timing

Facts

You own a beautiful but unreliable watch which loses exactly 8 minutes every hour. It is now showing 4:15pm. You know that it was correct at midnight when you set it, and you also know that it stopped one hour ago.

Challenge

What is the correct time now?

A 16

The time now is 7.45pm.

How to work it out

The clock is losing 8 minutes every hour, so for every real hour which has passed, the clock will only have showed an advance of 52 minutes. The clock now shows 4.15pm, so it has moved forward 975 'clock minutes' since midnight:

16.25 hours x 60 minutes = 975 minutes

These are clock minutes, though, not real minutes. The 'exchange rate' of clock minutes to real minutes is 52:60. In real minutes, therefore, 975 clock minutes are:

975 x (60 / 52) = 1125 minutes

1125 real minutes is equal to 18 hrs 45 mins. That is how much time has elapsed from the time the clock was set (midnight) to the time it stopped one hour ago. Midnight + 18 hrs 45 mins brings us to 6.45pm. As the clock stopped an hour ago, the time now must be 7.45pm.

SCORE		3

Q17 Thank Goodness it's Friday

If today is Friday, what is the day that follows the day that comes after the day that precedes the day before yesterday?

A17

The day is Thursday.

How to work it out

Start from the end of the sentence and work backwards.

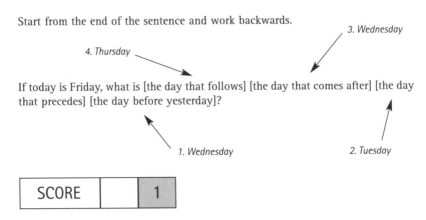

4. Thursday

3. Wednesday

If today is Friday, what is [the day that follows] [the day that comes after] [the day that precedes] [the day before yesterday]?

1. Wednesday

2. Tuesday

SCORE		1

Q18 Friends reunited

Hamish went back to the remote Scottish village where he was brought up and met an old school friend he had not seen for years. His friend said, "I am married now but not to anyone you know. This is my daughter".

Hamish turned to the little girl and asked for her name. She said, "I have the same name as my mother".

"Then you must be called Margaret," said Hamish.

He was right, but how did he know?

A 18

His old school friend was a girl - called Margaret.

SCORE		1

Q19 Ten stacks of coins

Facts

You have ten stacks of ten coins. One stack contains coins that weigh 1.1 grams each. The other nine stacks contain coins that weigh 1.0 grams each. The coins all look the same. You also have a set of weighing scales.

Challenge

Using the scales only once, locate the stack with the 1.1 gram coins.

A19

Take 1 coin from the first stack, 2 coins from the second stack, 3 from the third, and continue up to 10 coins from the tenth stack. Put all the coins together on the scales. If the total weight is 55.1g, the first stack had the heavier coins, if 55.2g the second stack had them, if 55.3g the third did, and so on up to 56g which would mean they were in the tenth stack.

Reasoning

By taking 1 coin from the first stack, 2 coins from the second, 3 from the third, and so on up to 10 coins from the tenth stack, there will be 55 coins in total: 1 + 2 + 3 + 4 + 5 + 6 + 7 + 8 + 9 + 10 = 55. If all coins weighed exactly 1g, then the total weight would be 55g. But we know that coins from one of the stacks weigh a bit more – 1.1g.

- If the heavy coins were in the first stack, from which you took just 1 coin, the extra weight overall would be 0.1g, making the total weigh 55.1g.
- If the heavy coins were in the second stack, from which you took 2 coins, the extra weight would be be 0.2g, making the total weigh 55.2g.

The same reasoning applies for every other stack, up to the tenth stack, where the extra weight would be 1g (10 x 0.1g), and which would make the total weight 56g.

SCORE		4

Q20 A confidence booster

(The question no-one gets wrong!)

Add the following numbers out loud, in order, and as quickly as you can:

1,000 + 40 + 1,000 + 30 + 1,000 + 20 + 1,000 + 10

Memorise the total, then turn the page to confirm that you can do basic maths.

A 20

The sum of the numbers is 4,100.

If you thought the numbers added up to 5,000, deduct 2 points from your score!

SCORE		1

Q21 Snails

Facts

A snail is climbing up a 10 foot pole. It climbs up by 3 feet every day at a consistent speed. Each night it sleeps. While sleeping, it slides down by 1 foot.

Challenge

Precisely when does the snail reach the top of the pole?

A₂₁

The snail reaches the top of the pole two thirds of the way through the fifth day.

How to work it out

The naive answer is that the snail climbs a net of 2 feet per day, so it reaches the 10-foot mark *at the end of* the fifth day. However, on the morning of the fifth day, the snail starts out at the 8 foot mark (having slid down from the 9 foot mark overnight). Two thirds of the way through the fifth day, it reaches the 10 foot mark and stops because there is no pole left to climb.

SCORE		2

Q22 Pure genius

If a genius-and-a-half can drink a fifth-and-a-half of a glass of Guinness in an hour-and-a-half, how many geniuses would it take to drink two fifths in 45 minutes?

A 22

Four Guinness-drinking geniuses would be needed.

How to work it out

We are told that a genius-and-a-half can drink a fifth-and-a-half of a glass in an hour-and-a-half. A fifth-and-a-half is equal to three tenths, so, restated, this statement is:

'A genius-and-a-half can drink three-tenths of a glass in an hour-and-a-half.'

in which case:

'Three geniuses can drink three tenths in 45 minutes'

which means that each genius can drink *one tenth* in 45 minutes. The number of geniuses required to drink *four* tenths in 45 minutes is, therefore, four.

| SCORE | 3 |

Q23 Burning on a short fuse

Facts

You have a string-like fuse that burns in exactly one minute. The fuse is inhomogeneous, and it may burn slowly at first, then quickly, then slowly and so on. You have a match, but no watch.

Challenge

How, using just the fuse and the match, do you measure exactly 30 seconds?

Reproduced from *Heard on the Street* with the permission of Timothy Falcon Crack

A 23

What is going to happen if you light both ends simultaneously? The two fizzing sparking flames are going to burn towards each other and meet. When they meet 60 seconds worth of fuse will have been burnt in two sections that each took the same amount of time. How much time? It has to be exactly 30 seconds because they both took the same time, and these times add to 60 seconds. Of course, you have to bend the fuse so that you can light both ends simultaneously and when they meet it probably won't be in the centre of the fuse.

SCORE		3

Q24 Tricky relations

If Teresa's daughter is my daughter's mother, what am I to Teresa?

- her grandmother
- her mother
- her daughter
- her granddaughter
- I *am* Teresa

A 24

I am Teresa's daughter.

SCORE		1

Q25 U2

Facts

U2's concert starts in 17 minutes and all the band members have to cross a bridge to get to the stage. It's your job to get the four men to the other side safely, and on time. Unfortunately, they cannot just walk over together. Because of the age of the bridge, only two people can cross at a time. To make matters worse, it is an evening concert, there is no moonlight and there is only one torch. The torch has to be used when crossing the bridge and it has to be walked back and forth; it cannot be thrown. Each band member walks at a different speed and if a pair walks together it has to walk at the rate of the slower man. Bono takes 1 minute to cross, Edge takes 2, Adam takes 5, Larry takes 10. If, for example, Adam and Larry walk across first, it would take them 10 minutes to cross. If Adam then returns with the torch, a total of 15 minutes will have passed.

Challenge

Decide in what order to send the men across the bridge, and who should make the return journeys with the torch, to ensure that they all get to the other side within 17 minutes, in time to play the concert. (Note: You cannot walk across yourself. Your job is just to organise the band members.)

A 25

The order that will get the band across in 17 minutes is:

Action	Time taken	Who's over the bridge?
Bono and Edge cross the bridge	2 minutes	Bono and Edge + torch
Bono returns with torch	1 minute	Edge
Adam and Larry cross torch	10 minutes	the bridge	Edge, Adam and Larry +
Edge returns with the torch		Adam and Larry
		2 minutes
Bono and Edge cross the bridge	2 minutes	Bono, Edge, Adam and Larry + torch
Total	*17 minutes*	

SCORE		4

50

Q26 Gallons

Facts

You have a tap running unlimited water, a three gallon container and a five gallon container.

Challenge

How can you measure exactly 4 gallons? (You are allowed to empty the containers down the drain.)

A26

The sequence you need to go through is as follows:

Action	Container A (3 gallons)	Container B (5 gallons)
Fill container B	0	5
Fill container A from B	3	2
Empty container A	0	2
Fill container A from B	2	0
Fill container B	2	5
Fill container A from B	3	4
Empty container A	0	(4)

This leaves 4 gallons in container B.

SCORE		3

Q27 More clocks

Exactly how many minutes is it before eight o'clock, if 40 minutes ago, it was three times as many minutes past four o'clock?

A 27

It is 50 minutes before 8 o'clock. 40 minutes ago it was 30 minutes past 6 o'clock, which is 150 minutes past 4 o'clock. At that time, the number of minutes by which it was past 4 (150) was three times as many as the number of minutes before 8 o'clock (50).

How to work it out

What we're looking for is the time now, expressed as a number of minutes before 8 o'clock. Let's call this number x.

If we convert 8 o'clock to 'minutes after 4 o'clock', it is 240. And the time now, expressed as minutes before 8 o'clock, is therefore 240 - x.

We are told that 40 minutes ago, the time was 3 times as many minutes after 4 o'clock as x. Since we've based 4 o'clock as 0 minutes, this can be expressed in an equation:

Time now - 40 minutes	=	Three x No. of minutes which 'now' is before 8 o'clock
(240 - x) - 40	=	3x
reducing to 4x	=	200
x	=	50

Q28 Lending library

Facts

The local library decided to give some of its old books to its 1,400 regular borrowers. To each of its female borrowers it offered 6 books and to each of its male borrowers it offered 4 books. Only half of the females and three quarters of the males took advantage of the offer.

Challenge

How many books did the library give away?

A28

The library gave away 4,200 books in total. You could work this out in two ways:

Trial-and-error

Assume that of the 1,400 regular borrowers, 1,000 were female. Half of them accepted the offer, which means the library gave away (500 x 6) books = 3,000 to females.

If 1,000 of the 1400 borrowers were female, 400 were male. 300 (three quarters) accepted the library's offer, and received 4 books. So 1,200 were distributed to males.

The number distributed was therefore 3,000 + 1,200 = 4,200.

Try the same calculation using 700 women and 700 men, and you get: (350 x 6) + (525 x 4) = 4,200, and the same goes for any other gender split.

Algebraic

f is the number of female borrowers
m is the number of male borrowers
n is the number of books given away

We know (1/2 x f) females, and (3/4 x m) males accepted the offer. Therefore, we know:

$n = 6 \times (1/2 \times f) + 4 \times (3/4 \times m)$
$n = (3 \times f) + (3 \times m)$
$n = 3 \times (f + m)$

We also know that the total number of borrowers is 1,400 $(f + m) = 1,400$.

Substituting 1,400 for $(f + m)$, we get:

$n = 3 \times 1,400$
$n = 4,200$

Q29 Two wheels good

Facts

Last week, Barry bicycled from Penzance to London following a route which was chosen for its beauty rather than its directness. On Day 1, Barry travelled a quarter of the total distance. On Day 2, he travelled half of the remaining distance. On Day 3, he travelled three quarters of the remaining distance. On Day 4 he travelled a third of the remaining distance. Barry now has 21 miles left to go until he reaches London.

Challenge

How far is it from Penzance to London, using the route Barry took?

A 29

The route Barry used is 336 miles long.

How to work it out

Assume the total distance is d.

Day	Distance ridden	On the day	Cumulative	Remaining
1	Quarter of the route [.25d]	.25d	.25d	.75d
2	Half of remaining distance [.5 x .75d]	.375d	.625d	.375d
3	Three-quarters of remaining distance [.75 x .375d]	.28125d	.90625d	.09375d
4	Third of remaining distance [.33 x .09375d]	.03125d	.9375d	.0625d

We are told that at the end of Day 4 Barry has 21 miles left to bicycle. If $.0625d = 21$, then $d = 21/.0625 = 336$

SCORE		2

Q30 Names for children

Mary's father has 5 daughters. The first 4 are called:

- Sante
- Senti
- Sinto
- Sontu

What do you think the fifth one is called?

A 30

The fifth daughter is called Mary.

If you answered 'Sunta', *deduct* two points from your score!

SCORE		1

Q31 Hats

Facts

Inside a dark closet are five hats: three blue and two red. Three intelligent men go into the closet, and each selects a hat in the dark and places it unseen upon his head. Each man knows that the closet contains three blue hats and two red and that the other two men have the same knowledge. Once outside the closet, no man can see his own hat. The first man looks at the other two, thinks, and says, "I cannot tell what colour my hat is". The second man hears this, looks at the other two, and says, "I cannot tell what colour my hat is either". The third man is blind. The blind man says, "Well, I know what colour my hat is".

Challenge

What colour is the blind man's hat, and how does he know?

A31

The only way the first man can know the colour of his own hat is if he sees the other two wearing red hats - of which there are only two. However, the first man does *not* know his hat colour, so the other two must be wearing either both blue or one red and one blue.

The second man, upon hearing the first, knows then that he and the third man are either both wearing blue hats, or one wears a red hat and one a blue. If he still does not know what colour hat he is wearing, it must be because the third man is wearing a blue hat. Why? Well, if the third man wears red, then that pinpoints his own hat as blue since this is the only option left from the choice of either both blue, or one red and one blue.

Since the second man does not know his hat colour, then the third man must be wearing blue. The third man, upon hearing the first two, deduces that his own hat is blue via the same reasoning.

SCORE		5

Q32 Analysts

Facts

One analyst (John) is talking to another (Mary) while working on a deal book at 2a.m. Mary learns that John's sister has three children. "How old are the children?" asks Mary. "Well," replies John, "the product of their ages is 36." Mary thinks for a while and says, "I need more information". "Hmmm, the sum of their ages is the same as this figure right here," says John pointing at the spreadsheet. "Still not enough information," says Mary after thinking for a minute. "The eldest is dyslexic," says John.

Challenge

How old are the children?

A32

John's sister's children are 2, 2 and 9. To work this out, first calculate all the possible combinations which could, when multiplied together, equal 36:

Age 1	Age 2	Age 3	Product	Sum
1	2	18	36	21
1	3	12	36	16
1	4	9	36	14
1	6	6	36	13
2	2	9	36	13
2	3	6	36	11
3	3	4	36	10

Which one is it? Well, Mary knows the sum (though we don't) and these potential siblings sum to 21,16,14,13,13,11 and 10 respectively. Knowing the sum was not sufficient for Mary to get the answer, it must be a non-unique sum. 13 is the only non-unique sum, so Mary knows that the children are either aged (1, 6 and 6) or (2, 2 and 9). John says *the eldest* is dyslexic, so there must be an eldest. That leaves 2, 2, and 9.

SCORE		5

Q33 The wrong outlook

Dennis was watching a late night film on television. Just after it finished at 12a.m., the weather forecast came on. "Torrential downpours continue to cause floods in the South East," said the presenter, "and it will continue to rain for the next two days. However, in 72 hours most of the South East will be bright and sunny."

"Wrong again," snorted Dennis.

He was correct to be so dismissive of the forecast, but how did he know it was wrong?

A 33

In 72 hours it would be midnight again, so it could not be bright and sunny.

SCORE		1

Q34 Funny money

Three executives check into a cheap hotel. They pay £30 to the manager and go to their room. Two minutes later, the manager realises that the room rate is only £25 and gives £5 in one pound coins to a hotel porter to take up to the guests. On the way to the room the porter decides to award himself a tip. He pockets two of the £1 coins, and gives one £1 coin to each of the guests.

The net result of these transactions is that each guest has paid £10 and got back £1, meaning they have paid £9 each - a total of £27 paid. The porter has £2, which, added to £27 makes £29. Where is the missing pound?

A 34

There is no 'missing £1'. Each guest paid £9, making a total of £27. The manager kept £25 of this and the porter £2. The other £3 from the original £30 paid was returned to the guests.

The porter's £2 should be added to the manager's £25 or subtracted from the guests' £27, not added to the guests' £27.

SCORE		2

Q35 A real turn on

Facts

A motel room has a single light in it. Outside the room, there are 3 light switches. The door of the room is closed, and you have been told correctly that the light inside is off, though you cannot see that from outside the room.

Challenge

Assuming that:

- The bulb and electrics all work fine.

- You can flick any of the switches any number of times.

- You can only open the door and go into the room once.

How can you determine which light switch operates the light inside the room?

A35

You can determine which switch turns the light on as follows:

- Leave switch 1 alone.
- Flick switch 2 for 1 hour, then flick it back.
- Flick switch 3.
- Enter the room.

If the light is on, then it was turned on when you flicked switch 3.

If the light bulb is warm but not illuminated, then it was turned on when you flicked switch 2.

If the bulb is neither warm nor illuminated, the light is operated by switch 1.

SCORE	5

Q 36 Running the bath

Facts

Your bath has two taps and a plug hole. The cold tap on its own is capable of filling the bath in 18 minutes, the hot one in 15 minutes. The plug hole can drain the bath in 10 minutes with the taps off.

Challenge

How long will the bath take to fill if you leave both taps on with the plug left out?

A36

It will take 45 minutes to fill.

How to work it out

If the cold tap can fill the bath in 18 minutes (3.33 baths per hour), and the hot one can fill the bath in 15 minutes (4 baths per hour), then together they would be able to fill 7.33 baths per hour, *with the plug in*.

With the plug *out*, it's a different story. The plug hole drains one bath in 10 minutes, or the equivalent of 6 baths per hour.

Putting the filling and drainage rates together, you would fill 1.33 baths (7.33 - 6) in one hour. The time it takes to fill just one bath (not 1.33) is therefore:

60 minutes / 1.33 = 45 minutes.

SCORE		2

Q37 A race against time

Facts

Assume that you're a commuter who drives to work. This morning, the traffic was so bad that you only managed to average 30mph on the outward journey.

Challenge

How fast will you have to drive home tonight, along the same route, to average 60mph for the entire round trip?

A 37

Sadly, it is impossible for you to average 60mph for the round trip, however fast you drive home.

Don't believe it?

Assume that the commuting distance is 30 miles. If you averaged 30mph on the outward trip, it would have taken you one hour. The challenge is to average 60mph for the round trip (out *and* back) but since you have already taken one hour on the outward trip, it is an impossible challenge.

Still not convinced? Let's suppose that for the return trip you took a ride on Concorde and averaged 900mph. You would cover the 30 miles home in 2 minutes. Your total trip time would be 62 minutes: 60 for the outward journey, 2 for the back. 60 miles in 62 minutes is very nearly 60mph, but not quite. *It can't be done!*

SCORE		2

Q38 Ahoy there!

Two Frenchmen were passing the time of day at St Tropez admiring Paul Allen's yacht which was moored in the harbour. One was a local fisherman, the other a Parisian banker. Over the stern of the boat hung a rope ladder with rungs 25cm apart, and with 3 metres showing above the water. The fisherman commented that the tide was just about to start rising and said that when it did it would rise at a consistent rate of 30cm per hour. He asked the Parisian how many metres of the rope ladder would still be above water after 5 hours of the rising tide. Can you help the banker?

A38

Still 3 metres because the ladder will rise with the ship!

SCORE		1

Q39 The bank interview

Facts

As part of its recruitment process, a City bank sits two promising graduates, Ruthless Rowena and Greedy Grant, in a closed room. The interviewer produces three stickers, two white and one black and shows them to the candidates. Upon each of their foreheads he places one sticker, so that neither candidate can see their own sticker or the unused sticker, but each can see the sticker on the other's forehead. He tells them that the candidate who is the first to correctly identify the colour of their own sticker will be given the job. After a few minutes, Ruthless Rowena shrieks with triumph and announces correctly that she has a white sticker. She gets the job.

Challenge

Assuming that Ruthless Rowena did not guess, and assuming that Greedy Grant is a clever individual, how could she possibly have deduced that she had a white sticker on her forehead?

A39

Rowena reasoned that if she was wearing a black sticker, then Grant would deduce that he must have a white sticker, on the basis that only one black sticker existed and if she was wearing it, he wasn't. Since Grant did not make that deduction, she reasoned that she must have a white sticker on her forehead.

Note that for this test to work fairly, the bank has to put white stickers on both candidates' foreheads. If it puts a black sticker on one candidate, the other candidate can immediately deduce that he/she has a white sticker because only one black sticker exists.

With both candidates wearing white stickers, neither is better placed than the other to work out the colour of their own sticker. In the example above, Grant could have made exactly the same deduction as Rowena.

SCORE	.	4

Q40 Mr Red

Facts

Everything Mr Red owns is red. He lives in a red bungalow with red chairs and red tables. His ceiling, walls and floors are red. All of his clothes are red, his shoes are red, even his carpet, television and phone are red.

Challenge

What colour are Mr Red's stairs?

A40

Mr Red doesn't have any stairs because he lives in a bungalow.

SCORE		1

Q41 Inside traders

Facts

Noticing a suspiciously large share trade just before the announcement of a takeover, investigating authorities decided that the trader must have been tipped off by one of the five directors who knew about the deal. The directors were interviewed, and, under pressure, each volunteered information. Their statements were:

James said:	a) it wasn't Tarquin	b) it was Basil
Tarquin said:	a) it wasn't James	b) it was Rupert
Basil said:	a) it wasn't Rupert	b) it wasn't Tarquin
Rupert said:	a) it wasn't Simon	b) it was James
Simon said:	a) it wasn't Basil	b) it was Rupert

Challenge

Assuming that exactly 5 of the 10 assertions above were true, and the other 5 were false, who committed the crime?

A 41

Simon committed the crime.

How to work it out

The way to work this out is by trial and error. Assume that one (*any* one) of the directors committed the crime, then go through the statements and add up how many of them are true. Only if Simon committed the crime are 5 of them true:

James said:	a) it wasn't Tarquin (**TRUE**)	b) it was Basil (**FALSE**)
Tarquin said:	a) it wasn't James (**TRUE**)	b) it was Rupert (**FALSE**)
Basil said:	a) it wasn't Rupert (**TRUE**)	b) it wasn't Tarquin (**TRUE**)
Rupert said:	a) it wasn't Simon (**FALSE**)	b) it was James (**FALSE**)
Simon said:	a) it wasn't Basil (**TRUE**)	b) it was Rupert (**FALSE**)

SCORE		3

Q42 Musical chairs

If the Manchester Quartet can play Schubert's String Quartet No.14 in 36 minutes, how quickly can the Birmingham Trio play it?

A42

Also in 36 minutes. The time it takes to play does not depend on the number of players!

SCORE		1

Your score

Congratulations! You've reached the end. If you got all the answers right using the correct reasoning, you could have scored 115 points. Add up the number you got, and read your assessment below.

0-39 points

Oh dear! You have a brain made of tofu, and are completely incapable of logical thought. It is said that a fool and his money are easily parted. The mystery in your case is how they ever came together.

40-79 points

Better! There are still worrying gaps in your education, and you are basically innumerate, but that need not be a problem. As long as you have no ethical hang-ups, a rewarding career in fund management awaits you.

80-99 points

The good news is that you have excellent powers of analysis and deduction. The bad news is that making money is as much art as science. Being clever is no guarantee of wealth.

100+ points

Nice to have you with us, Prof. Hawking!

Corporate purchases

Logic Problems for Money Minds is used by many companies as a light-hearted but effective way to assess the aptitude of job candidates. If your company would like to buy A4 printed test papers of the questions only (with answers on separate sheets), please contact us on enquiries@harriman-house.com.

Harriman House also offers the book's content in electronic quiz format, allowing candidates to complete answers online in a supervised environment and for scores to be recorded. If you are interested in this, please email us as above.

Heard on the Street

Readers who have enjoyed this book and who want to test themselves on harder material, are referred to *Heard on the Street* by Timothy Falcon Crack.

Heard on the Street is designed specifically to help candidates prepare for job interviews with banks and includes many of the questions which crop up year after year. More details of the book can be found by typing 'heard' into the search box at:

www.books.global-investor.com/bookshop

You can order the book from the same website, or phone Global-Investor on

+44 (0)1730 233870

Harriman House Titles

Taming the Lion
100 Secret Strategies for Investing
by Richard Farleigh

Richard Farleigh reveals the 100 secret strategies that he developed to enable him to succeed in the markets.

ISBN: 1897597622, Hardback, 224pp, 2005, Code: 21815, RRP: £12.99
www.harriman-house.com/tamingthelion

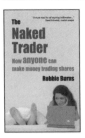

The Naked Trader
How anyone can make money trading shares
by Robbie Burns

In this revealing new book, top trader Robbie Burns cuts through the jargon to give you the lowdown on the strategies you need to make money from share dealing.

ISBN: 1897597452, Paperback, 276pp, 2005, Code: 19682, RRP: £12.99
www.harriman-house.com/nakedtrader

Fundology

The Secrets of Successful Fund Investing

by John Chatfeild-Roberts

In this important new book, an award-winning manager at one of the UK's best fund management firms explains in simple language what it takes to buy and sell investment funds successfully

ISBN: 1897597770, Hardback, 166pp, 2006, Code: 22930, RRP: £16.99
www.harriman-house.com/fundology

The Book of Investing Rules

Invaluable advice from 150 master investors

Edited by Philip Jenks and Stephen Eckett

Never before has so much quality advice been packed into a single book. If you want to increase your wealth through investing, this is an unmissable opportunity to acquire knowledge and skills from the best in the world.

ISBN: 1897597215, Paperback, 502pp, 2002, Code: 14870, RRP: £19.99
www.harriman-house.com/rules

Harriman House

Harriman House is a specialist publisher of books about money, investing and trading. The books listed are just a few of our titles, and they can all be bought through your local bookshop, direct from www.harriman-house.com by phone on:

+44 (0)1730 233870

If you would like a copy of our catalogue containing details of all our books, please call us on the same number, email us on enquiries@harriman-house.com, or write to Harriman House, 43 Chapel Street, Petersfield, GU32 3DY. We will send you our latest catalogue by return post.

Global-Investor

Harriman's sister company, Global-Investor, runs the well-known online bookshop of the same name:

www.global-investor.com/bookshop

The Gi Bookshop stocks more than 10,000 titles from over 200 different publishers. We enjoy a reputation for keen prices, friendly service and quick delivery, and have many individual and corporate customers worldwide. Next time you are thinking of buying a finance book, please try us out. We'd like to welcome you as a regular customer.